WHAT IS ART?

And

DOES IT EVEN MATTER?

Written & Illustrated by
Deborah Bradbury

Acknowledgements:

I want to express my sincere gratitude to my remarkable husband, who has consistently been by my side, giving me the nods and coffees throughout my entire writing journey. Your insights, encouragement, and contributions have been invaluable to me, shaping this endeavour into something extraordinary.

Special thanks to Carolina Herranz-Carr for her meticulous attention to detail and exceptional editorial expertise. Her discerning eye, unwavering professionalism, patience, and enthusiasm made the entire process a pleasure. She elevated this book in ways I never imagined, and I am deeply grateful for the care and dedication she brought to every page.

For my mother,
who planted the seeds of energy
and creativity in me.

I wrote this book to help children feel confident expressing themselves through art, to explore how artists use creativity to share feelings and ideas, and to discover that art can help us learn about others and the world. Still, it can also simply be fun, joyful, and a way to play with colours, just to see what they might become.

Deborah Bradbury

This book belongs to:

Hi! I'm Coco, and creating art is where I love to be,
every line and colour tells a story only I can see.

In these next few pages,
I've taken famous styles and made them mine.

You might spot a few you know,
with hidden hints in each design!

What stories do you think they show?
There's so much more than you may know.

But what is art… and does it even matter?
For some it's calm … for others, it's **CHATTER!**

So come along with me and let your imagination play.

Turn the page and let your vision lead the way!

...Claws,
what do I need you for
when I have wings to fly?
Coco the Crow

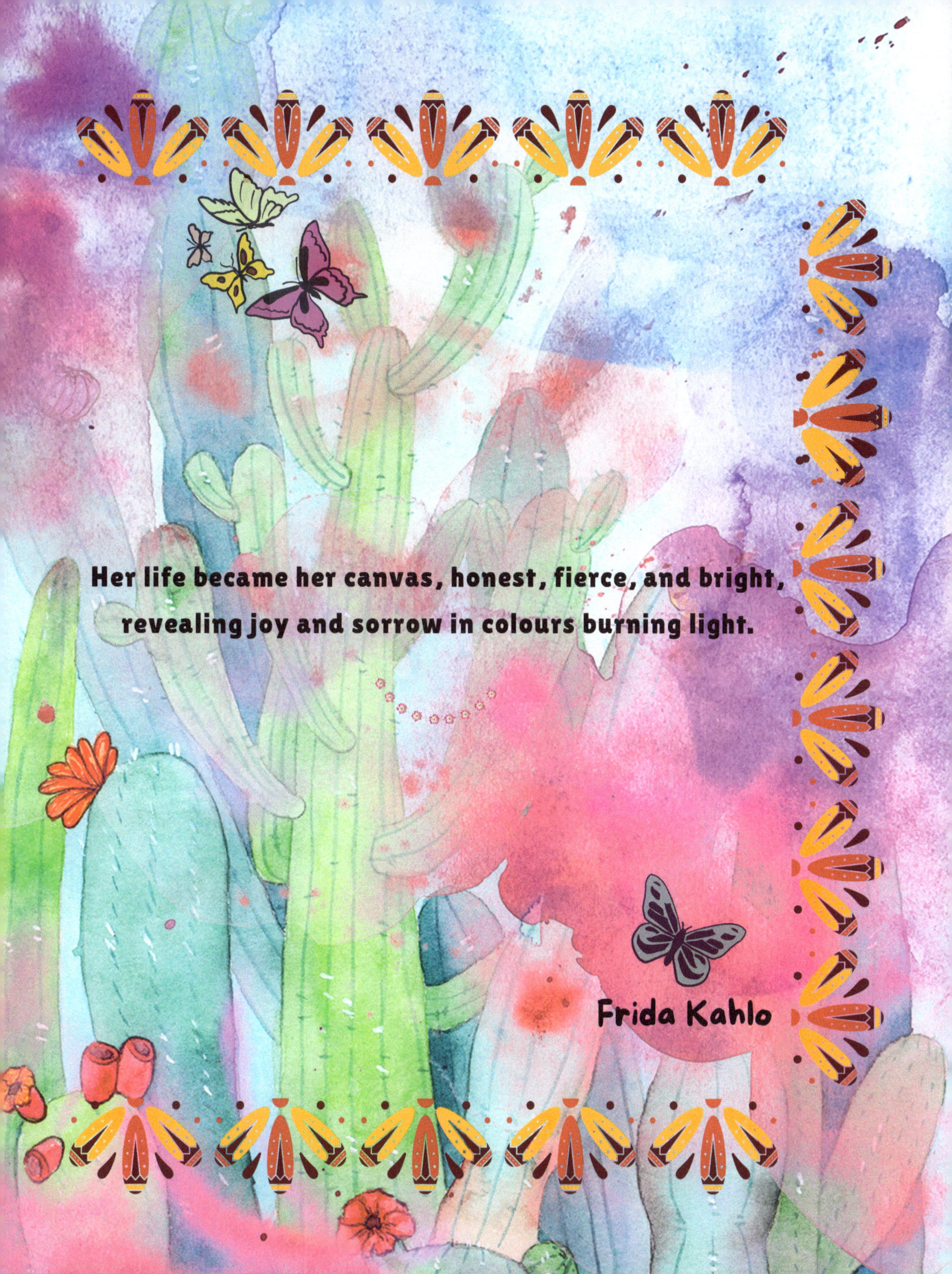

Her life became her canvas, honest, fierce, and bright,
revealing joy and sorrow in colours burning light.
Frida Kahlo

Coco the Crow

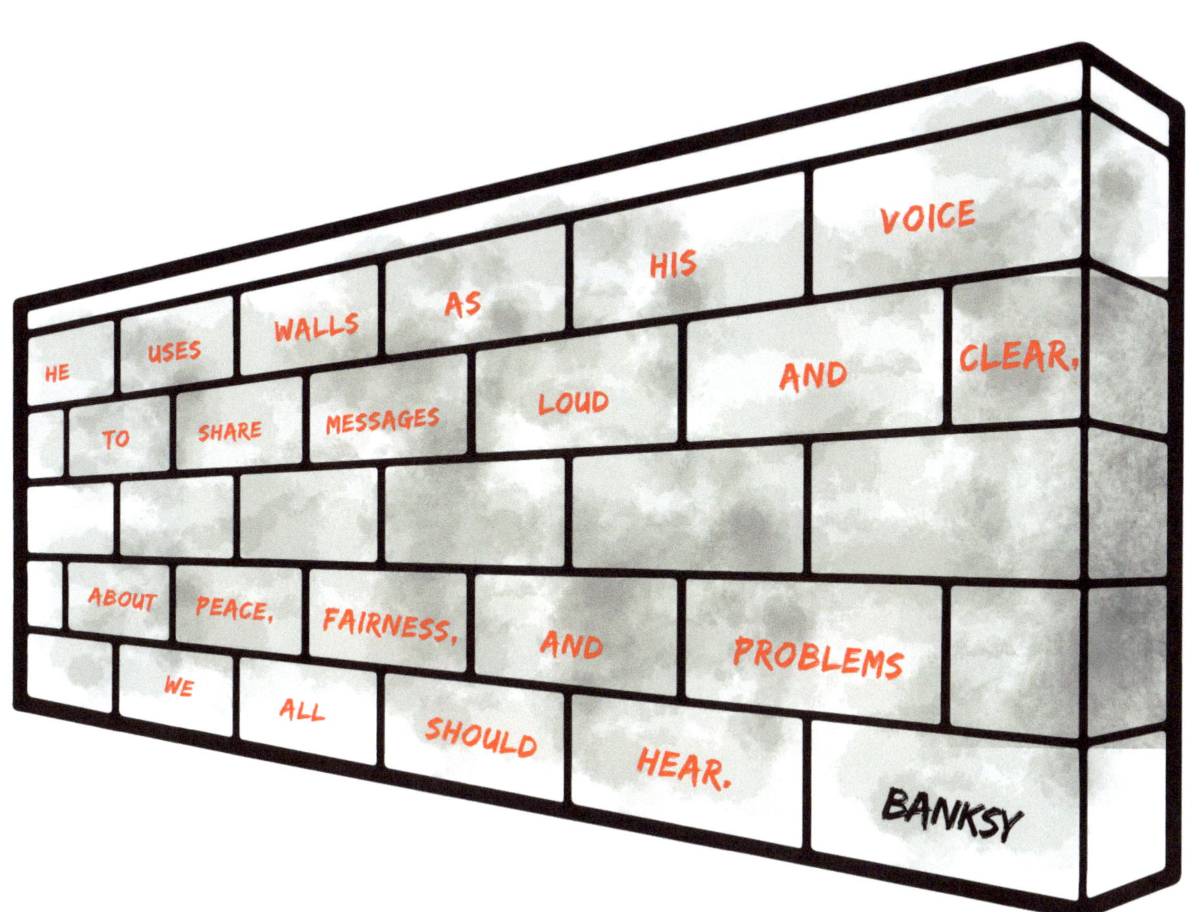

HE USES WALLS AS HIS VOICE
TO SHARE MESSAGES LOUD AND CLEAR,
ABOUT PEACE, FAIRNESS, AND PROBLEMS
WE ALL SHOULD HEAR.
BANKSY

HER ARTWORK IS RICH AND LIVELY AND BOLD.

Coco the Crow

SHE SHOWED THAT CREATIVITY IS FOR EVERYONE, YOUNG OR OLD.

'Alma's Stripes'

"EVERYTHING IS BEAUTIFUL"

Alma Thomas

50
50

Coco the Crow

HE USED ICONIC IMAGES AND EVERYDAY STUFF TO MAKE POP ART FUN TO SEE,
HOPING HIS PICTURES WOULD SPREAD JOY AND MAKE EVERYONE FEEL FREE.

In the future, everyone will be famous for 15 minutes.
Cola
Sam
X 25
SOUP
Inspired by
POPE OF POP
ANDY WARHOL

He painted smoky streets and crowds with kindness in his view,
because he cared about the people and the lives they struggled through.

He painted Salford's "smokey" tops... boxes from the shops... On cardboard

"The Big Ship Sails on the Alley-Alley-O"

THE ILLUSTRATIONS ON THIS PAGE
WERE INSPIRED BY THE SONG
"MATCHSTALK MEN AND MATCHSTALK CATS AND DOGS"
BY BRIAN AND MICHAEL– 1978
(A HEARTFELT TRIBUTE TO THE ARTIST L.S LOWRY.)

Twisted angles,
Colours glowing
Coco the Crow

Fresh new Styles
MALAGA
Every child is an artist!
I want to
paint something
new and
different!
Picasso
kept growing and growing

For me, at times, art does not matter,
because sometimes I just like seeing paint...

SPLATTER!

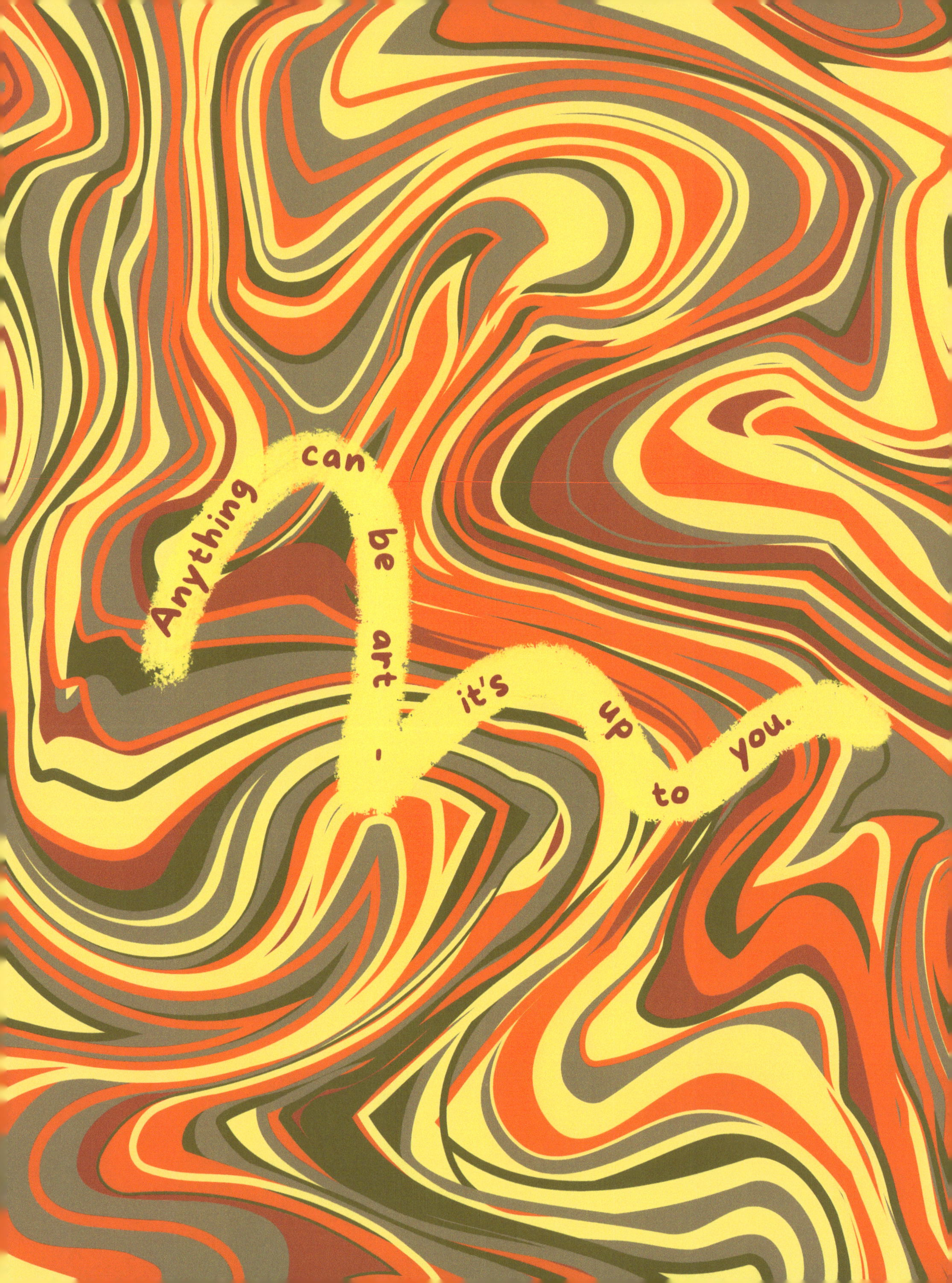

Anything can be art - it's up to you.

The world is full of wonders to explore and view.

BUT I LOVE PAINTING NATURE,
WILD MOUNTAINS SO FREE,

JUST DREAMING OF
SOARING
MAKES ME CALM AS CAN BE.

Spring feels refreshing as the world wakes up new,
fresh life, fresh sounds, fresh smells, shining through.

I love to paint the sunset,

glowing soft and low,

It says goodbye till morning,

then away again we go.

WHEN I FEEL SOLITARY, SCARED, OR SAD,

SHADOWY TONES SETTLE SOFTLY ON MY PAD.

WHAT DOES ART MEAN TO YOU?

WHAT STORY WILL YOUR ART SHINE THROUGH?

WHICH STYLE OF PAINTING DID YOU LIKE THE MOST?

COULD YOU TAKE INSPIRATION AND CREATE YOUR OWN POST?

FUN

FACTS

FRIDA KAHLO

Date of Birth	6 July 1907
Born in	Coyoacán, Mexico
Style & Tools	Colourful, emotional self-portraits using oil paint on canvas
Most Famous Artwork	The Two Fridas
Most Expensive Artwork Sold	$54.7 million (USD) in 2025

BANKSY

Date of Birth	Unknown (anonymous artist)
Born in	Bristol, England
Style & Tools	Street art using spray paint and stencils
Most Famous Artwork	Girl with Balloon / Love Is in the Bin
Most Expensive Artwork Sold	£18.6 million (GBP) in 2021

ANDY WARHOL

Date of Birth	6 August 1928
Born in	Pennsylvania, United States
Style & Tools	Pop Art using bright colours and silkscreen printing
Most Famous Artwork	Shot Sage Blue Marilyn
Most Expensive Artwork Sold	$195 million (USD) in 2022

L.S LOWRY

Date of Birth	1 November 1887
Born in	Stretford, England
Style & Tools	Scenes of everyday life using simple shapes and oil paints
Most Famous Artwork	Going to the Match
Most Expensive Artwork Sold	£7.8 million (GBP) in 2022

PICASSO

Date of Birth	25 October 1881
Born in	Malaga, Spain
Style & Tools	Cubism and modern art using oil paints and sculpture
Most Famous Artwork	Guernica
Most Expensive Artwork Sold	$179.4 million in 2015

Date of Birth	22 September 1891
Born in	Columbus, United States
Style & Tools	Bright, colourful paintings using dots, stripes, and shapes.
Most Famous Artwork	Resurrection
Most Expensive Artwork Sold	$3.9 million in 2023

Date of Birth	10 September 1945
Born in	Manchester, England
Style & Tools	Scenic views of the Cantabrian lakes & mountains using digital art (Ipad)
Most Famous Artwork	The Morning Sunrise
Most Expensive Artwork Sold	£1.60 (GBP) in 2027

Other books by this author!

Collect the Courageous, Clever Crow Picture Books Now!

ABOUT THE AUTHOR

Award-winning author Deborah Bradbury draws on over fifteen years as a primary school teacher and the joys of raising four children to create stories that are both educational and delightfully fun. A passionate advocate for reading, she is dedicated to inspiring young readers to develop a lifelong love of books.

Born in Manchester, UK, Deborah now lives by a scenic lake in Northern Spain, near a forest where friendly crows often visit. Life in Cantabria with her husband, their cats, and playful dog Spike inspires many of her book illustrations. Fluent in two languages, she enjoys cycling and playing squash in her free time.

Author page ⤳  Scan for free downloads!

 https://www.deborahbradburybooks.com    @bradbury_books    @DBradburyBooks